First published in Great Britain by
Pendulum Gallery Press
56 Ackender Road, Alton, Hants GU34 1JS

© TONI GOFFE 1995

TV WATCHING
ISBN 0-948912-34-0

All rights reserved. No part of this publication may be reproduced or transmitted in any form or by any means, electronic or mechanical, including photocopying, recording, or any information storage and retrieval system, or for a source of ideas without permission in writing from the publisher.

PRINTED IN GREAT BRITAIN BY
UNWIN BROTHERS LTD, OLD WOKING, SURREY

YOU DON'T HAVE TO BE CRAZY TO WATCH T.V. —BUT IT HELPS...

IN A RECENT SURVEY, IT WAS STATED THAT SOME PEOPLE ARE WATCHING AS MUCH AS SIX HOURS OF TELEVISION A DAY...
    WITH THE HELP OF THIS BOOK, IT IS HOPED THAT YOU WILL BE ABLE TO EXTEND THIS BY FOUR HOURS, TO AN INCREDIBLE TEN HOURS PER DAY......HAPPY VIEWING......

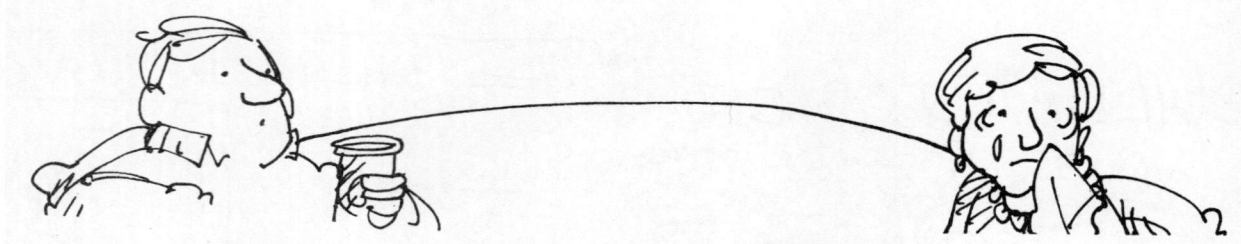

THERE ARE ALWAYS PERIODS OF TIME WHEN YOU ARE WATCHING TV THAT YOU CAN LOSE INTEREST AND FALL ASLEEP.

COMMERCIAL BREAKS OR SOMETIMES THE PROGRAMMES BETWEEN THE COMMERCIAL BREAKS ARE THE PERIODS I MEAN, OR THE "SOPPY BITS" IN FILMS THAT YOUR PARTNERS CAN OFTEN BE FOUND CRYING IN......

THIS BOOK WILL HELP YOU FILL IN THESE PERIODS IN A CONSTRUCTIVE AND INTERESTING WAY........ HAPPIER VIEWING.

BE A CAT BED....

PLAY HIDE AND SEEK...

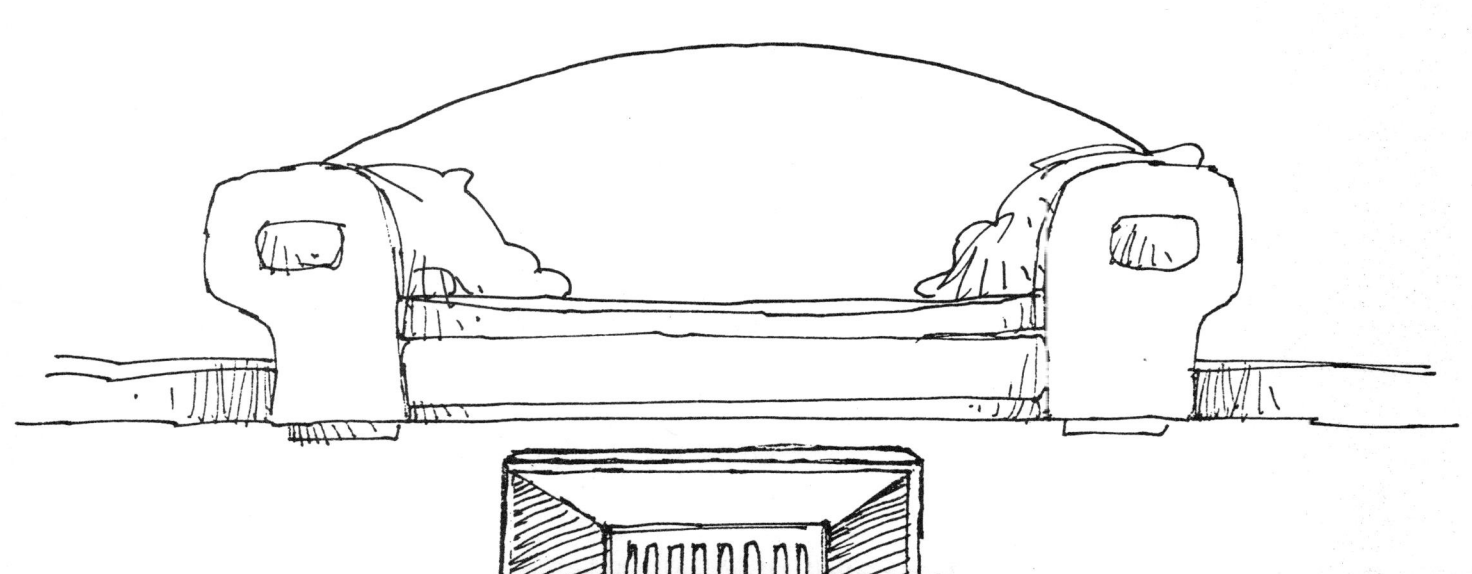

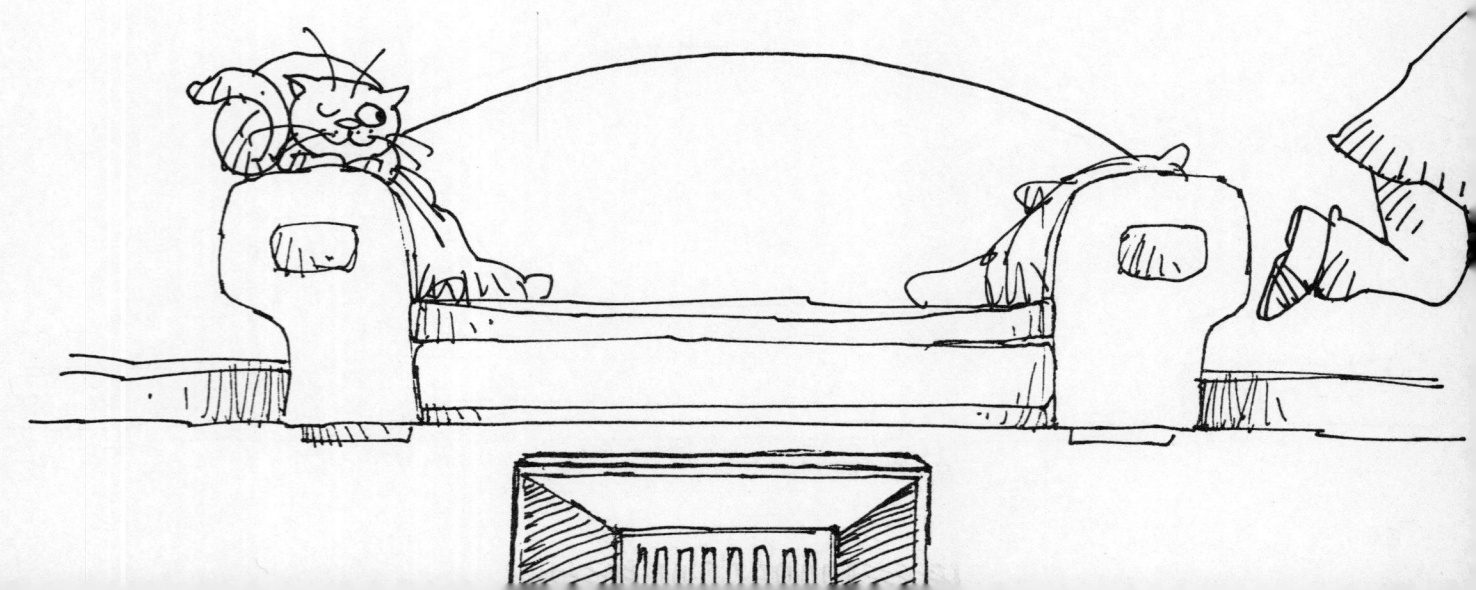

PLAY WITH YOUR CHILDREN...
...SOMETIMES...

HAVE A NICE QUIET FAMILY EVENING VIEWING...

TRY BODY-BUILDING EXERCISES...

RELIVE YOUR YOUTH, START A PILLOW-FIGHT!!

GET INVOLVED WHEN YOU WATCH RUGBY...

PLAY CHARADES...

CHECK TO SEE IF YOUR ROOM IS BIG ENOUGH TO SWING A CAT...

SURPRISE A VISITOR WITH YOUR TARZAN IMITATION...

TRY THIS NEW WAY TO WATCH AN OLD FILM... YOU'VE SEEN BEFORE

CHEER UP YOUR FAMILY WHEN THEY ARE WATCHING A "WEEPY" FILM...

SIT THROUGH A SCARY FILM WITHOUT CLOSING YOUR EYES....

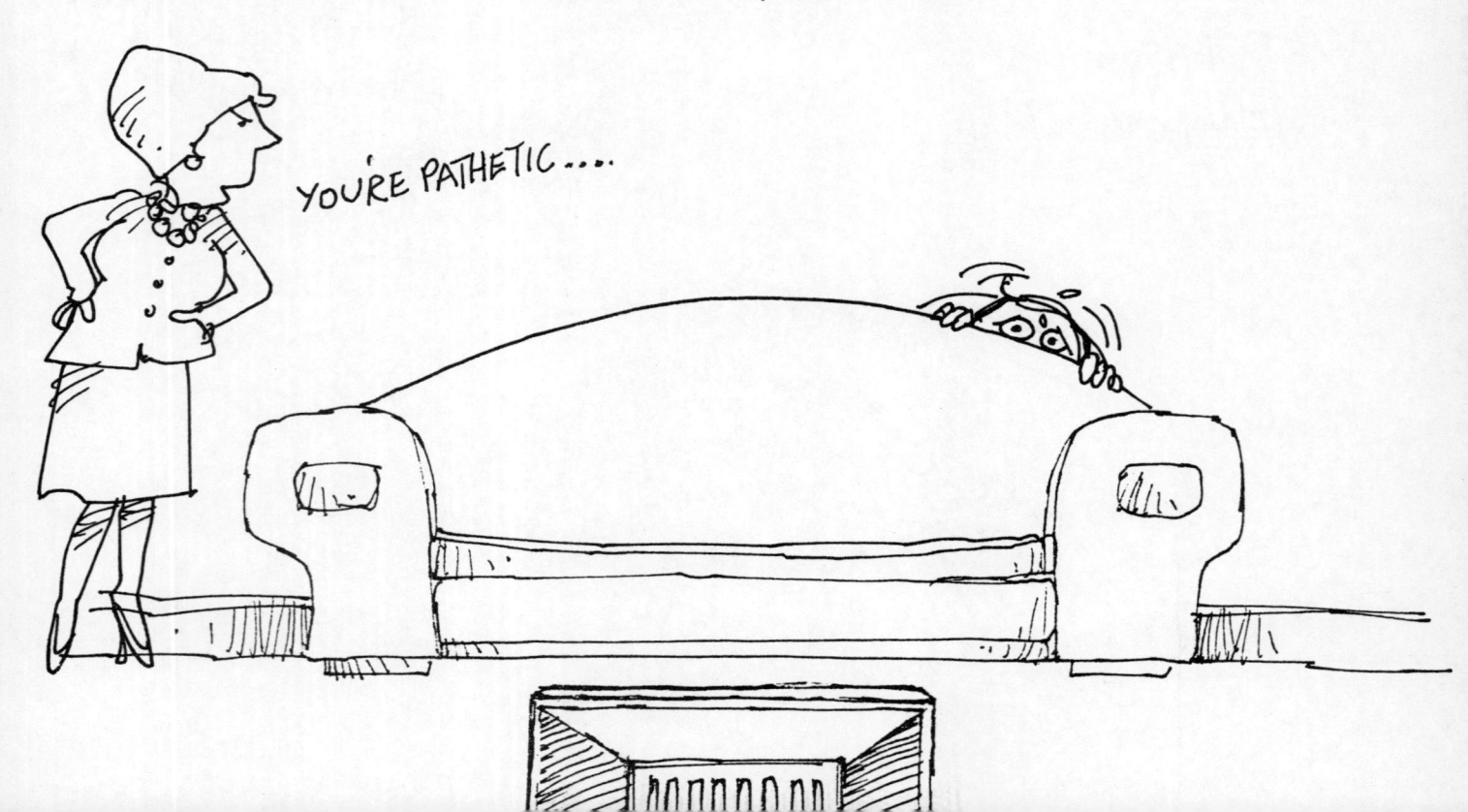

YOU'RE PATHETIC....

MAKE SCARY FILMS _REALLY_ SCARY!!

WOMEN CAN ALSO BE 'COUCH POTATOES!'... GIVEN THE OPPORTUNITY...

TRY TO FOLLOW THE AEROBIC PROGRAMMES....

THE WONDERFUL THING ABOUT TV IS THAT YOU CAN WATCH AND DO THE HOUSEWORK AT THE SAME TIME...

PRACTISE THE SPLITS...

INVOLVE YOURSELF IN THE COOKING PROGRAMMES....

WHEN DEPRESSED, WATCH A NICE BLACK AND WHITE FILM... INDULGE YOURSELF....

TAKE YOUR BABY FOR A WALK....

WHEN IN A HURRY, LEAVE THE TV SWITCHED ON, AND VIEW AS YOU PASS....

HAVE A PICNIC WITH A FRIEND....

A LITTLE TRAPEZE WORK CAN ENHANCE AN OTHERWISE DULL TV EVENING...

TRY A CLIMBING EXPEDITION....

OR SKYDIVING....

TRY WOOD CARVING;
MAKE A TOTEM
POLE...

...AND COUCH JUMPING...

OR CAR MAINTENANCE.....

SEX CAN BE FUN TOO....

COUNT HOW MANY LATE NIGHT FILMS YOU HAVE SEEN THE END OF.....

...AND SO TO BED....

PENDULUM GALLERY PRESS

56 Ackender Road·Alton·Hants·GU34 1JS Fax & Telephone Alton (0420) 84483

SPORT

		IBSN NO
JUDO FOR JUNIORS	£2.99	0.948912.01.4
JUDO GAMES	£2.99	0.948912.00.6

HUMOUR

IS THERE SEX AFTER 40 FOR HER?	£2.99	0.948912.20.0
IS THERE SEX AFTER 40 FOR HIM?	£2.99	0.948912.19.0
ARE YOU FINISHED AT 50?	£2.99	0.948912.05.7
ARE YOU STILL FLIRTY AT 30?	£2.99	0.948912.06.5
THE VERY VERY SEXY ADULT DOT-TO-DOT BOOK	£2.99	0.948912.09.X
THE NEW SEX DIET	£2.99	0.948912.04.9
SEX AND YOUR STARS	£2.95	0.948912.08.1
HAPPY? BIRTHDAY	£2.99	0.948912.12.X
HAPPY? RETIREMENT	£2.99	0.948912.10.3
GET WELL SOON	£2.99	0.948912.15.4
FARTING!	£2.99	0.948912.17.0
GREENS ARE GOOD FOR YOU	£2.99	0.948912.13.8
CAN SEX IMPROVE YOUR GOLF?	£2.99	0.948912.18.9
IS THERE LIFE WITHOUT DOGS?	£2.99	0.948912.22.7
IS THERE LIFE WITHOUT CATS?	£3.99	0.948912.21.9
IS THERE LIFE AFTER 60?	£2.99	0.948912.24.3
IS THERE LIFE AFTER BABY?	£2.99	0.948912.23.5
IS THERE A LIFE LEFT FOR GRANDPARENTS?	£2.99	0.948912.25.1
WAS THERE LIFE BEFORE COMPUTERS?	£2.99	0.948912.26.X
WHY WHY D.I.Y.?	£2.99	0.948912.29.4
LIFE'S LESSONS FROM MY CAT	£2.50	0.948912.27.8
LIFE'S LESSONS FROM MY DOG	£2.50	0.948912.28.6
LOVE CATS	£2.50	0.948912.30.8
THINGS MEN DO TO REALLY ANNOY WOMEN	£2.99	0.948912.31.6
THINGS WOMEN DO TO REALLY ANNOY MEN	£2.99	0.948912.32.4

TO BUY THESE BOOKS YOU CAN EITHER ORDER FROM YOUR LOCAL BOOKSELLER OR FROM US AT PENDULUM GALLERY PRESS·56 ACKENDER ROAD·ALTON·HANTS·GU341JS· (PLEASE SEND £1 EXTRA TO COVER POSTAGE AND PACKAGING)